YOUR ISSUES NOT MINE

Psychological Projection (Healing My Inner Child)

BY

MARY WROTEN

Contents

DEDICATION 3

ACKNOWLEDGEMENTS 5

INTRODUCTION 7

CHAPTER 1 9

UNDERSTANDING PSYCHOLOGICAL PROJECT 9

CHAPTER 2 16

I'VE BEEN ROBBED 16

CHAPTER 3 25

THE VISIT 25

CHAPTER 4 35

DREAMS, DREAMS...MY PAIN 35

CHAPTER 5 45

FORGIVING YOUR CHILDHOOD ABUSER 45

CHAPTER 6 50

EMOTIONAL WALLS 50

CHAPTER 7 56

LOW SELF-ESTEEM/COMPARING OURSELVES TO OTHERS 56

CHAPTER 8 62

RE DISCOVERING YOURSELF 62

CHAPTER 9 69

CHANGING YOUR THOUGHTS 69

THE END.... 76

DEDICATION

To God, my Father and Lord and Savior Jesus Christ, Thank you for guidance and strength throughout my life. All who are struggling with childhood trauma,

May this story offer a beacon of hope, reminding you that you are not alone, and healing is possible. My daughter, Evelyn: You are God's gift to me. Grandson, Joziah: Your innocence of joy reminds me of the beauty in the world and the resilience of the human spirit.

Brenda Candelario, Words fail to capture the depth of my gratitude for your unwavering support. You saw the real me, flaws and all, and never wavered in your care. Thank you for the gift of your acceptance. Lisa Gattis, Your support means the world to me. You always had been a patient listener, offering understanding and helped me to see things through different lenses…Thank you. Dianna Miranda: I sincerely appreciate your incredible support. Your ability to listen, understand and guide me towards different perspectives has been instrumental in my growth.

To my dearest inner child, you have blossomed into a radiant butterfly. The walls you once built as protection have crumbled, replaced by a garden of growth and possibility. Thank you for embracing change and refusing to remain trapped in fear. I'm so proud of your courage to seek change and break free from the confines of the past.

ACKNOWLEDGEMENTS

I would like to extend my deepest thanks to the following individuals, whose support throughout this journey has been invaluable: Asif Ali, I want to express my sincere gratitude for your incredible work on the cover design for my book "Your Issues Not Mine" You perfectly captured the essence of the story, and the cover is both eye-catching and visually appealing. Annie T, I want to take the moment to express my gratitude for your amazing work on "Your Issues Not Mine". Your insightful edits and guidance have truly elevated the manuscript, and I couldn't be happier with the results.

Brenda Candeleria, Dianna Miranda and Lisa Gattis: Your support and helpful critiques of the book cover were essential to this project. Marina Brown and Valerie Grayson: Thank you for reading the book and offering your honest perspectives. This book would not have been possible without all of you. Your contributions have made a world of difference.

Bonnie William, I would like to extend my heartfelt gratitude to you, for your efforts in editing, format, and refining my manuscript were invaluable. Your dedication and expertise played a significant role in shaping this book into its final form."

"Fall in love with taking care of yourself. Fall in love with the path of deep healing. Fall in love with becoming the best version of yourself but with patience, with compassion, and respect to your journey."

-S. Mcnutt

INTRODUCTION

We all retain echoes of our past inside us. Our childhood experiences, like skipping stones across a pond's surface, cause ripples that influence our perceptions, feelings, and behaviors. This book invites you to investigate the fundamental relationship between these early imprints and how we navigate life and the world as adults. Psychological projection, a subtle yet powerful force, frequently serves as a lens through which we see the world.

Unconsciously, we project our own unresolved emotions and desires on others. This can result in misunderstandings, confrontations, and erroneous perceptions of reality. At the center of these projections is the wounded inner child a part of us that yearns for love, validation, and safety. By responding to our inner child's wounds, we can develop self-compassion, establish stronger relationships, and reach our greatest potential. This is more than just a journey of self-discovery; it is a path to freedom, allowing us to break free from past patterns and embrace a more real and fulfilled existence. We will begin a healing process for the injured inner child through self reflection, mindfulness practices, and focused therapeutic procedures. Through this investigation, we may delve into the complexities of psychological projection, discovering how it emerges in our relationships, careers, and self-perception. We will journey deep to meet the wounded inner child, discover its roots, and how it affects our daily life.

This book invites you on a transformative journey to uncover the complex relationship between psychological projection and the inner child. We will investigate the origins of these early traumas and how they manifest in our adult life through the prism of projection. From minor distortions in our perceptions to open disagreements in our relationships. It is time to give in and meet the child within that yearns for love and affection. By cultivating this inner garden, we can live a life of wealth, connection, and fulfillment. Are you prepared to start on this transformative journey?

CHAPTER 1

UNDERSTANDING PSYCHOLOGICAL PROJECT

Psychological projection, what is that? Projection refers to unconsciously taking unwanted emotions you don't like about yourself and attributing them to someone else. One example is a cheating spouse who suspects their partner of being unfaithful. Instead of accepting responsibility for their infidelity, they project it onto their partner. In other words, 'It's not me, it's you." Why do we project? Projection, like so many other facets of human conduct, boils down to self-defense. According to Koenig, projecting what you don't like about yourself onto someone else shields you from having to face unpleasant aspects of yourself. She goes on to say that people do more at ease perceive undesirable features in others than in themselves.

From the perspective of a parent, projection is particularly problematic since it can lead to children adopting ideas and behaviors to keep "living up" or "living down" to a projected identity. Consider this awful example of a mother who grew up believing she would never be able to achieve her goals or establish herself among her peers.

This mother may tell her daughter that life is unfair and that she should

Not expect to achieve great things. This is a clear projection, because the mother, not the child, is the one who feels like a failure. The mother, unable to cope with her emotions, unwittingly passes them on to her daughter. After years of hearing negative projections, the daughter may be ready to act.

This subjection to a projected identity is particularly painful because it effectively deprives the child of her own identity and prospects. It may appear that the youngster should understand that her mother's statements are only a mirror of her own life. Unfortunately, most children are unable to make such judgments. Instead, they prefer to absorb these projections into their own identities. Even when youngsters can reject negative projections, disagreement between them and their parents is common. In many cases, animosity develops, and youngsters have a strong desire to leave home and break up with their parents.

On the other hand, the projection could have a positive connotation and might encourage children to think positively about themselves. A high-achieving parent may unconsciously reflect ambition and confidence onto their children, assisting in the development of a more positive self-image that leads to success. However, this can also show as excessive pressure, making the youngster feel like a letdown for not meeting the parent's expectations. It's not uncommon for parents to project their unresolved difficulties onto their children because they usually have unconscious urges. Even the most loving parents might unconsciously project their anxieties, frustrations, prejudices, and expectations onto their children. Even in the greatest of conditions, this can have an impact on children's development, leading to them adopting identities that aren't necessarily their own.

Consider your childhood and whether you adopted your parents' assumptions into your own identity. How does it affect and impact your internal and external selves, emotional and mental states as well as your relationships with others? Author Anais Nin once said, "We don't see things as they are, we see them as we are," pointing back to psychological projection. What is real? In other words, our experiences from the cradle to adulthood shape our identity. According to Maslow (1943), self-actualization is achieved when our basic needs are met. When there is a deficiency, we fail to reach self-actualization, in turn, we will more than likely engage in psychological projection. Maslow considers these as lower-level needs.

Which Include;

- **Basic Physiological Needs**: Things vital to survival (e.g., air, food, water, warmth, sleep).

Safety Needs: Things that give people control over their lives (e.g., shelter, financial security, personal health, and wellness).

- **Love Needs:** Social interactions (e.g., friendships, family relationships, romantic partners, interactions with community groups).
- **Esteem Needs:** Interactions that give a sense of appreciation and respect, both from an individual's community as well as their self-esteem and sense of accomplishment.

Maslow referred to lower-level needs (physiological, safety, love/belongingness, and esteem) as "deficiency needs" (or "D-needs"). He notes that deprivation in any of these categories will motivate behavior to resolve that deficiency. For example, individuals whose emotional needs (e.g., love and affection) were not met as children will be motivated to address that deficiency by seeking out people to fulfill that need even if it's a negative relationship. The longer an individual is lacking in a D-need, the hungrier they are, and the more motivated they will be to rectify the deficiency to find food. Therefore, self-actualization is not based on the lack thereof, but on what an individual needs to become. The deficiency in these needs leads to psychological projection instead of self-actualization.

"Before we can free ourselves from the darkest depths of hell that has become our everyday reality…. we must first find the courage to peer fearlessly at the darkness that lies within.

For only then can we finally begin to walk our path towards healing, recovery, and self-discovery."

-Shirley Alexis Johns

They were never my issues… How and why, this happened.

"If you want to understand your parents more, get them to talk about their childhood; and if you listen with compassion, you will learn where their fears and rigid patterns come from. Those people who did all that stuff to you were just as frightened and scared as you are."

- Louise L. Hay

CHAPTER 2

I'VE BEEN ROBBED

Our primary caregivers are our parents. We look to them for love, affection, support, affirmation, and care. We expect them to comfort us when we are terrified and to soothe us when we fall or are injured. We have no fears as youngsters since we know our parents or guardians will always be there for us. In a supportive and encouraging environment, we develop a positive self-image, healthy emotions, mental health, confidence, and social skills as youngsters.

As a result, we mature into emotionally and mentally healthy adults in society. Unfortunately, many children suffer from emotional neglect and deprivation during their youth. As kids get older, they will eventually create an internal map of how the world works based on the trauma they have experienced. As a result of emotional neglect and deprivation, children grow up with an emotional deficit because they've been robbed emotionally. To know what emotional deficit entails, we must first grasp these terms: emotional neglect and emotional deprivation.

Emotional neglect and deprivation both include a lack of emotional attention and responses from parents and caregivers, but they occur in different settings and can have very different outcomes in children's lives as they develop into adulthood. Childhood emotional deprivation occurs when a youngster is denied emotional nourishment throughout his or her early years. It involves parents or caregivers who entirely disregard their children's needs for comfort, affection, and happiness. Additionally, physical, mental, and sexual abuse are examples of emotional deprivation. When a child's physical needs are met, but his or her emotional needs are not, it is known as an emotional deficit. As a result, the youngster is denied the opportunity to grow into a healthy emotional adult.

I can attest to having suffered from emotional deficit both as a child and as an adult. As a child, I had a bulging stomach from hunger, slurred speech, and burnt arms. In addition, I was confined to a dark closet and denied access to the bathroom. I was fed very little. After a month in the hospital, I was placed in foster care at the age of three due to serious maltreatment. At nine years old I was molested in one of my foster homes. Also, I went from one foster family to another four times, never bonding with anyone emotionally. Furthermore, I grew unhappy and sobbed every day because I felt so alone. No one could comfort me or make me feel safe and protected. I was completely depleted. I was denied the opportunity to mature emotionally. It was and continues to be difficult for me to express myself. Emotionally, I became a dysfunctional adult. I'm afraid to knock down the barriers I put up to keep people out. I wanted to be loved and to give love, but I couldn't because my invisible walls wouldn't let anyone in. I was alone, detached, and depressed. I believed I was the worst person on the planet at one point, but God protected and loved me, nevertheless. He became my best friend.

By the time I was 17 years old, I was reunited with my mother, who lived in Brooklyn. To my amazement, she had more children who were younger. I couldn’t understand how she had other kids but placed me in foster care. This added to my feelings of rejection and hurt. How could my mother hate me so much, but have other kids? I remember her telling me that I wasn’t the cutest in the family. Man, I felt hurt by that comment. How could a mother say that to her child, nonetheless, I was crushed, fell deeper and deeper into despair, and was emotionally wounded. In the summer, I would get up early and walk to New Lots Train Station to get on the train. I would sit in the corner and just cry. Late at night, I would walk the streets crying. I was trying to find a place where I could talk to God about my pain. I guess, I thought that my mother would love and accept me once I returned home, but that wasn't the case.

One time my sister Dolores found a court paper that stated that my mother denied me as her daughter. In the deposition, she said that I was the daughter of her mother's friend. When her mother died, I came to live with her. How could a mother deny her child? It was done to me. Another hit to my emotions…I was devastated. Finally, I asked her if she denied me and why. Her response was, "You came between me and my mother (my grandmother)." And when my grandmother died, she felt that I should be dead too. Then, she stated that she would do it again. Boy, it blew my mind!! Imagine the effect it had on my emotions and self-esteem. I was walking around alive but dead on the inside. No one could hear my silent cry.

Because of the abuse, I was left bankrupt in my emotions. I was an emotionally wrecked individual with a bad self-image of myself. I didn't allow anyone to get close to me for fear of being hurt and abandoned again. Because of my mother's insecurities and mindset, she projected her feelings onto me. Instead of nurturing me, she abused me emotionally, physically, and mentally, she wanted me dead. Why? I was denied being her daughter, why? The answer lies within her relationship with her mother, my grandmother. Based on stories from my aunts, my grandfather was abusive toward my grandmother. Since my grandmother was abused, most likely, she could not provide the love and nurturing my mother so needed. Unfortunately, my mother felt neglected emotionally and allowed her pain to inflict harm on me. As a result of her projection, I developed issues that would remain with me in my adulthood.

Even as an adult, I am still dealing with the residue of emotional deprivation and neglect. I have no real connection to anyone emotionally…I've been robbed. Can you imagine feeling alone in the world despite having a daughter and a grandson? I love them dearly, but they cannot fill the void in my wounded inner child who is longing to be loved. There is emptiness in my soul. I'm functioning, but I still, have a hole in my soul. However, I'm trusting God to heal me in my emotions. To heal my inner child that was robbed!!!The first step to healing is to acknowledge that you have issues.

It's not easy admitting to emotional hurt, but we must be our true selves. See, acknowledging hurt is the first step to healing. Accepting your vulnerability is not only part of the process of healing, but it's also one of the truest demonstrations of strength. Like a bone that heals to become stronger than it was before our emotional well-being improves with proper attention and care. This is a lot harder than it sounds because healing from emotional pain is more complicated than healing from physical pain. With physical pain, our bodies make sure that we feel and repair, while our brains often try to push aside any emotional pain.

This is so true; I remember one of my older sisters telling me that my mother held me over a hot tub of water in the bathroom. She heard me screaming and ran into the bathroom. I was found with both of my arms in the water. Of course, she quickly screamed at my mother to stop before my entire body emerged. For years, I believed I got the burn scars from standing on a stool and trying to reach for a box of grits from out of the cabinet to cook in a huge pot on the stove. I don't know if I was brainwashed to believe that or if my mind protected me from accepting the painful truth.

This may not be your story. Maybe you did not face abuse as a child but watched your father abuse your mother. A friend of mine once told a story about how she could not trust relationships with men because she watched how her father cheated on her mother. Maybe your parents or guardians had a problem with substance abuse and were unable to raise you. Any trauma experienced during childhood can continue to affect your life as an adult; therefore.

by:

It is necessary to identify the root of your problems by:

- Revisiting your childhood (this can be painful).
- Identify who caused you pain and hurt.
- Find out why (their state of mind or what was going on at the time the mistreatment started).
- Forgive.
- Express how you were made to feel.
- Cry if you must.
- Have a desire to be healed.
- Pray and ask God to help you.
- Write a letter to your wounded inner child.

We must protect ourselves from further deprivation of love, relationships, and self-esteem; broken but not finished. Remember healing is a process. There is no wound so deep that God cannot reach down and heal.

Beauty Doesn't Begin in the Mirror; It Begins in Your Heart.

The visit...Hi, I'm your inner child…nice to meet you.

CHAPTER 3

THE VISIT

When we reflect on our lives, we may wonder why we act the way we do, particularly if we have been abused by our parents or caregivers. It all begins in childhood, throughout the five phases of child development, which comprise infants, toddlers, preschool, elementary school, and adolescence. According to some psychologists, our human brain influences our cognitive and behavioral development in later life from birth through early childhood. In other words, our actions are shaped by how we were treated by our parents or caretakers.

We must explore our inner kid, even though it is uncomfortable at times, to comprehend our current habits. When we look back on our childhood, we can see how our parents projected their difficulties and issues onto us in the form of maltreatment and abuse. Reminiscing about our childhood would help us see that our problems are the result of our parents' inability to nurture and love us because they were unable to provide what they had not received as children. As a result, we grew up to be emotionally sick adults, retreating to our inner wounded child, who remained dormant in our subconscious. We absorb our feelings, mistreatment, family, ourselves, and society, as well as how we connect with others, in our subconscious.

Why is it vital to reconnect with your inner child? Connecting with your child allows you to explore the part of your personality that behaves and feels like a child. Things that happened to you while you were younger can leave a lasting impression on your mind. It's critical to reconnect with your inner child since it will assist you in healing, evolving, and blossoming as an adult. Recognize your inner child as the first step toward healing and rediscovering yourself. Furthermore, accept their presence with compassion and allow them to occupy space in your adult life. When we let our inner child emerge, it transforms our world, and we live a more fulfilling and happier adult existence.

We can begin to understand which negative belief systems stem from our upbringing and drive us to behave the way we do to certain people or situations by accepting this aspect of ourselves consciously. Everyone has an inner kid, but as we grow older, many of us unconsciously cut ties with our inner child. When our basic needs aren't addressed as children, our inner child is injured, and the subsequent patterns of behavior can hurt our self-esteem as adults, leading to unfulfilling personal relationships or the formation of self-destructive life habits. "The inner child represents an emotional state or a manner of being that is a vestige of the child that we once were," explains Dr. Venetia Leonidaki, a Clinical Psychologist and Psychotherapist. It's about the part of us that feels vulnerable, gets hurt or angered quickly, and acts rashly, but can also experience pure delight and be spontaneous, playful, and innocent.

We all have a child inside us because we were all once children. Connecting with your inner child allows you to react and explore the part of your personality that feels like a child. What happens when you are young can leave its mark on your mind. Inner child healing focuses on identifying and resolving the root cause of the childlike aspect of personality so that it can address future challenges as an adult, not as an injured child.

The concept of "inner child" helps to better recognize emotional needs. Otherwise, it can easily be dismissed as irrational and stupid. As children, we all have the same basic needs for security, love, verification, autonomy, spontaneity, and respect for boundaries. We have the same needs in adulthood, and if left unaddressed for extended periods, they can cause a variety of mental health problems. We need to learn to listen to and raise our inner children. Finding and meeting those core needs as much as possible gives us the best chance to enjoy the satisfaction and fulfillment of life. Ignoring or neglecting the inner child can lead to problems and feelings of discontinuity, or it can take over the urge and lead to self-destructive behaviors." - Dr. Venetian Leonidaki.

As we grow up, we lose access to the needs, pains, hopes, and dreams of our inner children, often ignoring who they are for the version of society we need. When we were small, we didn't care what was real and what wasn't. Reality and appearance are mixed like a carefree watercolor painting, where one day I will play at the end. We ignore the inner child to create a place for our adult life and the various expectations we must meet to be accepted.

Dr. Venetian Leonidaki said, "Early in life, we need to find a balance between the emotional needs we feel within ourselves, and the demands and restrictions imposed by others around us. Our parents, teachers, and later our partners, employers, and children demand that we take responsibility, control our emotions, be rational, and follow social norms. We always have internal needs. This often results in oppression and isolation from the inner child, as we have to negotiate with external pressure." Our desire to please other sand we must also ignore the inner child. The fear of losing their love. Neurobiology also plays a role. Changes in certain areas of the brain, such as the prefrontal cortex, bring new sophistication to our thoughts and make better preparations for coordinating emotions and urges. Our most sophisticated adult mindset is less dependent on the raw emotions that our inner child is primarily in contact with and may keep us away from our child's part.

There are ways to connect with your inner child if you're ready to embrace your inner child. There are five ways you can open your heart to that part of yourself with compassion and kindness. They are;

- **Be Creative:** To participate in artistic activities and games, you need to use your imagination, reduce your defenses, and use your emotions. You can try everything from artwork to pantomime performances to karaoke songs. Creative work unleashes our childhood qualities, including spontaneity, playfulness, ingenuity, and fun.

- **Contact with Children:** Spending a fulfilling time with children, including yours, will give you a direct experience of a carefree, but also very emotional state. It may also help you remember your childhood memories and feelings.
- Fall in love: Of course, you can't plan this, but when you're in love, you'll find that you're experiencing a variety of emotions similar to those you experienced as a child. Our growing need for affection and intimacy, jealousy, and separation anxiety are examples of emotional states that become stronger when we are in love and have a strong connection to childhood.
- **Explore Your Childhood Memories:** By closing your eyes and focusing on the details and sensory elements, you can guide your mind to the childhood memories that you can remember more clearly. What did we look like? Do you have a scent you remember? Looking at old photos, rediscovering childhood toys, and revisiting places you frequented as a child can also help with this task.
- **Please Consult the Therapist**: Having a therapist to guide you through this process can be very helpful. The therapist can help by pointing out

subtle or hidden emotions that may belong to that part of you. Some therapists use experiential techniques to bring out the inner child. One example is chair work, where you sit in a chair that represents your childhood and speaks from a child's perspective.

It's not always a fun job, but it can dig deeper into the feelings of the past and childhood and provide a new depth of self-awareness and understanding. This implies that the child within now has access to a deeper level of self-compassion by engaging in adult role playing and embracing who you are today. It can also redefine your thinking and teach you to keep a sufficient distance between your inner child and your present self.

Once you know where a particular emotion or "trap of life" is coming from, you can start healing your inner child and use it to heal your entire adult self. Your inner child can also unearth your forgotten parts and empower you in adult life to regain a sense of playfulness, creativity, optimism, and the joy of simple things. I can do it. By connecting with the Inner Child, you will be able to experience a wide range of emotions, increase your creativity, increase your desire for fun, and feel more at ease.

Dr. Leonidaki Venice noted, “By connecting with the inner child, you will be exposed to a wide range of emotions, increase your creativity, enhance your desire for fun, feel more reassured, and reduce emotional numbness, discontinuity, and mental health issues. You can notice suppressed negative emotions that may be more vulnerable to the problem. If you have childhood wounds that need healing, reconnect them with the inner child. You may have the opportunity to deal with it. Finally, connecting different parts of yourself may give you a more complete understanding of who you are. For those with unresolved trauma and difficult childhood memories, the idea of seeing the inner child again can be a catalyst.

Looking back on past events may even seem counterproductive but under the guidance of a therapist like Dr. Venetian Leonidaki, you can handle this painful and deep-seated emotion, meet the needs of the inner child, and give him/her the opportunity to be seen, heard, and loved by recognizing this vulnerable person. I will explain. Working on the healing of the inner child fosters self-esteem and makes it possible to express those suppressed emotions healthily.

This is a rewarding and painful process, so expert help can be very important to help people experiencing trauma recognize vulnerable inner children. Fostering compassion within yourself also helps to weaken the power of inner critics. Inner critics can easily offend, dismiss, or humiliate an inner child in an inner dialogue. Helping the inner child meet the needs for the first time in life and taking responsibility for raising and raising the little boys and girls inside you is also part of the healing process.

Dr. Leonidaki Venezia states that "People with a history of childhood trauma often experience a high level of shame on their inner children and develop coping mechanisms aimed at curbing them. The first step to healing is to bypass such a mechanism and reconnect with the inner child. This includes reconnecting with the fears, sadness, loneliness, and abandoned emotions commonly found in people with a traumatic history.

For example, if you experience emotional negligence as a child, recognize how you feel and tell others to meet the unmet needs of emotional connections and validation. You may need to work harder as an adult to express yourself, so practicing life skills that you may not have had the opportunity to fully develop early in your life is your inner child. Increases the likelihood that your unique needs will be met.

My inner childhood fears through dreams (nightmares).

CHAPTER 4

DREAMS, DREAMS…MY PAIN

Recovering memories that have been suppressed for a long time can have a crippling effect on the trauma recovery process. They have been suppressed for a reason. When you experience significant trauma, the brain shuts down, dissociation takes over, and as a survival mechanism, the trauma(s) get unconsciously blocked and tucked away from you and stored into disorganized files in your brain because of a high level of stress, or you were in a situation where you felt threatened and it was a matter of life or death, so your mind did what it had to do to keep you sane.

When old memories resurface, they might change how you perceive yourself and your relationships. You may experience repressed memories in a variety of forms, such as triggers, nightmares, flashbacks, body memories, and somatic or conversion symptoms. Denial, humiliation, guilt, wrath, hurt, grief, apathy, and other negative emotions might result from your present circumstances, your relationships, and the people in them. This can send you back in time and keep you there, giving you the impression that the trauma is happening all over again. It may be followed by dissociation, depersonalization/ detribalization, and dissociative amnesia, which might destabilize you and your life. When you're locked in those memories, it can cause you to perceive "safe" individuals as "unsafe," and you might not even feel safe around yourself. This may result in feelings of alienation, avoidance, poor self-care, and internal conflict.

Your body may respond in ways that it did then, which may be unfamiliar to you and incredibly terrifying. When faced with what you consider to be insignificant situations, you can find yourself entering the fight, flight, freeze, flop, or fawn responses. Reenactment habits could reflect your memories accurately. You can observe yourself repeating actions connected to your traumas. Any way your memories resurface is legitimate. It doesn't matter how you and your body react when memories surface.

Your reactions to your recollections are normal, and everything is ok. You are presently safe and in good health. Establish a line between reality and your recollections, practice remaining rounded and, in the present, and permit yourself to be gentle to yourself throughout this process. Tell a reputable therapist about your experiences. Give yourself room to be vulnerable. Be kind and understanding to yourself. Recovery from trauma is not always a straight line; you might remember everything that happened to you. Even if you don't remember it, it can still have an impact on your subconscious. That's okay too if you only have a few blocks representing various traumas. When you're ready to cope with them, your suppressed memories will resurface to you. They are there to inform you what happened to you, to help you understand why things are the way they are, that it's time to work with them, and that you are safe enough to do so. They are not there to harm you or destroy the life you have built for yourself.

Oftentimes, experiences of abuse and trauma show up in our dreams. The classic definition of a dream is a mental sequence of sights, sensations, and thoughts that occur while a person is asleep. Additionally, sounds might be used to accompany this, which typically has a narrative character. It’s common to have nightmares and anxious dreams following a distressing incident because dreams frequently reflect what we see and feel when we're awake. Similar emotions and sensations to those felt during the trauma are frequently incorporated into the content of these disturbing dreams.

I remember dreaming about the man who molested me when I was 9 years old. In the dream, I would be running from my foster father while he chased me. I was running because I didn't want him to hurt me again. Finally, I had a dream that I stopped running in the dream. I turned around and faced him. Then I said to him, "God is not going to let you hurt me anymore." After that dream, I never had that nightmare again. I recently decided to rear my inner child again. I started having dreams about my youth while I conversed with my inner kid. In one dream, I kept hearing someone say, "I'm stupid." They repeatedly told me in the dream that I was stupid. "I'm not dumb, I'm smart," I said to myself.

When I first awoke, I became aware of how frequently I had been called stupid throughout my early years. Unfortunately, I had buried these phrases in my subconscious, and they stayed there for a long time. The amusing thing about this is that I used to think I wasn't smart enough when I was awake. The phrase "You're a moron" contributed to my behavior of feeling inferior.

I was traveling in a car with someone in another dream. Strangely, she was sitting on me while driving. She then informed me that she was working extra hours.

“Okay,” I said in response. When I woke up, the dream that I had experienced as a child and adult was clear to me. When I was awake, I frequently felt unappreciated and that no one ever chose me for any task. My self-esteem suffered greatly from feeling this way.

I noticed that I started becoming angry when my bosses refused to choose me for overtime. More than just overtime was at issue. I've always been ignored throughout my life. Select me, pick me, I cried. All of this occurred because I felt undervalued as a person. I was looking to be validated. Now that I am re-parenting my inner child, I have started to re-affirm her. I must let my inner child know that she is not in danger anymore, not alone and not bad.

Trauma survivors are frequently extremely driven individuals. For survival purposes, many people have been trained to be extremely observant and vigilant. Because they were held to unattainable standards by their abusers and their attempts to appease them frequently backfired, they are frequently excessively critical of themselves. Some end up being overachievers yet never feel like what they accomplish is sufficient. Some survivors stop trying because they know nothing will ever be good enough to please their abusers, allowing their abusers' lies about them to come true. When trauma prevents them from achieving their goals, rather than a lack of ambition, many survivors internalize the notion that they are "lazy." It's harsh to be told to "think positively." Anyone who is healing from psychological and emotional abuse, in other words, faces that exact difficulty. They are now struggling to maintain their sanity, to recover their thinking after someone else took control of their mind. Additionally, more than just their brain was hijacked. The physical body becomes programmed with emotional stress. It not only causes emotional suffering but also a great deal of physical discomfort, which can occasionally develop into a dangerous long-term sickness.

Positive thinking obscures the fact that people occasionally feel self-conscious. Survivors must lower their defenses and feel their emotions in order to heal. When a trauma survivor is under pressure to "think positively," this is the second issue. For a victim, this May frequently sound like it's inappropriate to feel whatever they are feeling, leading them to bury it and often consign it to their subconscious.

Those who have endured trauma are masters at hiding their emotions. Burying emotions, however, makes it harder for the survivor to get the resources they need to heal. Burying feelings does not make the agony go away. Dissociation is a common symptom of survivors. Confronting this experience is necessary for healing.

Like this, minimizing is crucial for coping, whether for the survivor or those close to them. Typically, both. It's not only difficult to heal when someone says, "It's not that awful," or "It's not as bad as Joe had it," but it's also difficult to recognize the trauma in the first place. As a result, when a survivor decides to "not sweat the small stuff," the little things balloon into an impassable mountain of suppressed sensations and emotions. More skeletons will be added to the subconscious skeleton pile if you develop a practice of not speaking up, whether it's to maintain peace or to avoid unpleasant emotions.

Many people would say let it go, if only it was that easy. If survivors could, they would do it without hesitation. Although this is the ultimate objective in trauma resolution, it frequently appears in front of the trauma survivor's face as some glimmering, enchanted object that is impossible to obtain. Too many people are attempting to move past trauma that they haven't quite processed. To release something, you must first be conscious of why you are holding it in the first place. Trauma that has been held in the subconscious mind's closed cabinets and closets and continues to rule from within, frequently without the survivor fully realizing what is happening. Before such issues are brought to the surface and dealt with in full, the process of letting go cannot begin.

It is not possible to let go unless such issues are brought to light and thoroughly dealt with. That again entails experiencing unpleasant emotions. It denotes mourning. It entails treating yourself with the kindness and consideration that no one else provided. Sometimes, it entails a brief period of moping. A survivor's severe inner critic typically doesn't permit this for very long. It entails rejecting the critic. To objectively assess the situation, entails bringing all of our unconscious thoughts into our awareness. It will take time for you to let go. As you re-parent, re-affirm, and cherish your inner child, take pleasure in this beautiful path of self-discovery.

As an adult who experienced abuse as a child, I have viewed myself through damaged lenses and believe that I am unlovable, foolish, and unattractive. Through my eyes, I could see nothing admirable about myself. I had the idea that I needed to be both pretty and smart in order to be liked and accepted. I seemed to be experiencing the same emotions on the inside as I was outside. I was walking around dead on the inside and had low self-esteem. I didn't love who I was. If my mother rejected me as her daughter, how could anyone love me? I was fighting to survive while in excruciating pain and wandering around dead within.

"Forgiveness is not always easy. At times, it feels more painful than the wound we suffered, to forgive the one that inflicted it. And yet, there is no peace without forgiveness."

- Marianne Williamson

The blame game… Learning to Forgive.

CHAPTER 5

FORGIVING YOUR CHILDHOOD ABUSER

The concept of "forgiveness" is fraught with ambiguity. We are required to forgive those who have wronged us because it is the proper thing to do. Many people mistakenly believe that showing forgiveness entails approving of the initial behavior.

No form of child abuse, including the pernicious emotional and psychological abuse perpetrated by parents, is ever acceptable. We cannot expect them to take responsibility for their actions since that is not how parents behave. They tend to blame others, externalize their problems, and lose touch with their feelings and actions. Due to this, it makes forgiving them harder.

There is an internal letting go for your well-being that enhances your mental health and emotions. As long as you don't minimize the harm and sorrow that was done to you and finds reasonable limits to prevent it in the future, forgiving in this way is healthy and healing. For adult children who experienced rejection, and physical, sexual, and psychological abuse, we can't justify poor parenting. The fundamental rights and needs of children cannot be disregarded. Therefore, forgiveness involves letting go of the past on an internal level, but only after working through your grief during your healing.

Other approaches to dealing with forgiveness may involve referencing one's spiritual and religious roots. According to the twelve-step addiction recovery programs, you can only truly forgive someone if you wish them well after they have wronged you. Twelve-steppers go one step further and hope that the person who wounded you has everything you want for yourself, including health, happiness, etc. The key issue is that the type of forgiveness you select completely erases responsibility, leaving you with no evidence of feeling like a victim. Because if you have a victim mindset, you run the risk of basing your entire existence on your injuries. We cannot listen to the wounded for advice!

We cannot allow the failures of others to control who we are. It's not easy to forgive, Hana Malik states that, "Forgiveness is taking the knife out your own back and not using it to hurt anyone else no matter how they hurt you." A quote by Henri Nouwen describes forgiveness thus, "Forgiveness is the name of love practiced among people who love poorly. The hard truth is that all of us love poorly.

We need to forgive and be forgiven every day, every hour, unceasingly. That is the great work of love among the fellowship of the weak that is the human family."One of the most challenging things is to forgive your parent or caregiver for the abuse. The biblical command is to forgive others. Has that made it ok? No. When someone harms us, understanding doesn't mean we approve of it. It signifies that we are aware. The secret to forgiveness is compassion and understanding.

The truth is that there must be reciprocity, in which the other acknowledges wrongdoing and apologizes, for forgiveness to be effective. This hardly ever seems to occur in the case of abusive parents. It might be difficult to forgive an abuser, particularly when that abuser was someone you should have trusted to love and guard you without condition. To forgive a parent who has wronged you requires a lot of courage. Whether you decide to include an abusive parent in your life right now, forgiving them can still help you get past it and recover.

I can recall writing a letter to my mother as a young adult. I informed her that I was sorry for the wrongs she had done to me. I handed the letter to her. In all honesty, I don't know if she ever read it. The letter received no response from my mother. If I could go on, I would be fine with it. I had to forgive everyone who had hurt me, including my sister and a foster parent who had assaulted me when I was a child. I recall coming to church by myself and staying in from noon till midnight. I spoke to God for a while. I prayed to God for guidance on how to completely forget those who have wronged me. I began singing hymns, including, to name a few, "Is Your Wholeness on the Altar,""Pass Me Not O Gentle Savior,""Blessed Assurance Jesus is Mine," and "Yes, Jesus Loves Me." I continue to sing and pray while crying. My tears were cascading down my face as I sang "Yes, Jesus loves." I then began to thank God for loving me and for giving me reasons to praise and worship him.

My heart began to suddenly be filled with God's love. God removed the pain, but I still needed to get my childhood trauma-related issues fixed. The abuse began when I was a little child. So, you see, forgiving someone is about you freeing yourself so you can move on in the healing process. Unforgiveness leads to bitterness and imprisonment of the soul. For that reason, it is essential to learn how to forgive; it is not easy, but necessary in the healing process.

"Stories live in our hearts. As we grow older, they retreated, deeper and deeper. We cover them with walls and shields and heavy armor, thinking we are protecting our hearts. But sometimes, the walls fall and the armor breaks, and one brave story would escape, flying out of the prisons of our hearts."

- Unknown

CHAPTER 6

EMOTIONAL WALLS

A universal human experience is having painful feelings. Throughout your life's journey, you have been hurt by harsh words or reprimanded by a parent or instructor who was not pleased with you. You might have experienced heartbreak or been deceived by a friend or partner. You started to construct emotional barriers to guard your heart as these experiences took place.

Over time, you learned that the ache of being harmed wasn't as bad, and your walls became taller, thicker, and stronger. During your childhood, you started to build your emotional walls. Perhaps you were in an unsafe environment where you experienced trauma, severe abuse, and neglect. You were made to feel unsafe to express your emotions.

You constructed barriers to better live and cope in your environment because of the trauma, and these walls have helped you to remain functional and prevent you from disintegrating. You try to shield yourself from showing how fragile you are by erecting barriers. After being harmed, being vulnerable feels so challenging. This topic was fully discussed in “The Power of Vulnerability: Teachings of Authenticity, Connections, and Courage” by Dr. Brene Brown. According to Brown,” When we feel vulnerable, we often experience negative emotions like dread, humiliation, and uncertainty. When we try to suppress these feelings, she contends, we lose sight of the fact that being vulnerable is also the "birthplace of joy, belonging, creativity, honesty, and love."

You may have felt extremely exposed to emotional harm when you started to raise your emotional boundaries. Emotional walls keep you from enjoying the beautiful aspects of life. In addition, it influences you to have low expectations of others and life. In other words, it can be difficult for feelings to get through your emotional barriers. Do not expect anything, and you will not lose anything. Right? You learn to cope with low expectations from others, and you choose not to express your feelings because doing so makes you feel too exposed. Though your walls have safeguarded you from the outside world, they also come with a personal cost.

Also, when you put walls around your heart, it's hard to feel other people's feelings, let alone your own, as you are overcome by a kind of emotional numbness. You may have trouble identifying your feelings about something. When you guard your emotions, you miss out on the beautiful parts of life, including vitality and passion. You also lose out on having a loving, connected relationship if you don't spend time with your partner.

There are several signs to examine to determine if you have built emotional walls:

- You don’t feel intense joy or deep sadness.
- In a relationship, your partner may doubt your love for them.
- You are an able manager of your emotions so you can minimize the discomfort you feel when your feelings go unexpressed.
- You engage in self-sabotage in your romantic relationships, ending the relationship before you can get hurt.
- People may have told you that you are “hard to read.”
- Living a single life might be your preference.

Do any of this sound familiar? Try to dig deep and explore if it might be possible that you are living behind emotional walls. Are your walls preventing you from forming a deep love connection or the ability to experience a vital and passionate life?

The following list of potent strategies can help you go through your emotional barriers and discover true love and connection:

- Find a reputable therapist.
- You can explore the causes of your potential emotional insecurity in relationships with the aid of a qualified therapist.
- You can learn how to ask for what you want and need to repair this childhood wound once you have discovered what is operating in your unconscious and subconscious mind.

Investigate the development of your emotional walls.

- You weren't concerned with your feelings being harmed when you were born. The armor for your emotions came later.
- You have the fortitude to deal with the discomfort while wearing it.
- Understanding the causes of your emotional walls and explaining them will help you gain perspective, self-compassion, and the capacity to

Increasing your resilience is a good idea.

- Increasing your resilience will enable you to recover from upsetting feelings.
- Rewriting your story using optimism in practice.
- Avoid personalizing it.
- Encourage others.
- Obtain stress relief.
- Push your comfort zone limits.

To start tearing down your emotional barriers, you must be committed and practice communicating your emotions in a setting where you feel emotionally comfortable. The loveliest parts of your life do not have to be missed. As you start to appreciate the worth and significance of self-expression, learn how to establish emotional safety, become more at ease with vulnerability, and form healthy expectations. You can reclaim a life lived fully, energetically, and passionately while also gaining the advantages of a close bond with your partner and those you love.

"The greatest discovery in life is self discovery. Until you find yourself you will always be someone else. Become yourself."

-Myles Munroe

"The reason we struggle with insecurity is because we compare our behind the scenes with everyone else's highlight reel."

CHAPTER 7

LOW SELF-ESTEEM/COMPARING OURSELVES TO OTHERS

Children who experience childhood abuse and trauma often develop a feeling of not being good enough. Unfortunately, they go through life comparing themselves to others because of the message they received from their parents that they are not worthy of love. Oftentimes, they develop low self-esteem in which they view themselves through damaged eyes. As a result of low self-esteem, they never reach their potential and therefore become stuck with their inner child. The most important things in life are internal not external. It is how we view ourselves on the inside. Comparing ourselves to others is like keeping a scorecard.

When we judge ourselves against others, they can control our actions. You and another person are compared in this kind of comparison. Sometimes it has to do with something genetic, like wanting to grow taller, but more frequently it has to do with a skill that the other person possesses that we wish we had. Perhaps Sally produces better reports than you do, and perhaps Bob enjoys a better marriage than you do. This comparison can be damaging or inspiring depending on the situation.

Except in cases where you are the best in the world, making comparisons with other individuals is a prescription for misery. Because, let's face it, only one person can fulfill that. The others are also upset, in addition to us. They are undoubtedly comparing themselves to you; perhaps they are envious because you are more skilled at networking than they are. In the worst-case scenario, when we compare ourselves to others, we find ourselves expending more effort on demeaning them than on uplifting ourselves. Being yourself is the one thing you do better than anyone else. The only game you can actually win is this one.

Many people get the belief that they are not good enough as they age. We may grow up thinking that we are never enough if we are treated cruelly as youngsters and made to feel unworthy or inadequate. Such a conviction is frequently the result of being held to unattainable ideals (perfectionism), compared to others, and treated unfairly in general. We develop the false beliefs that whatever we are doing is not good enough, that we always need to do more, that we can never relax, and many other false beliefs as a result of growing up with such a mindset.

Our mental health and general well-being depend heavily on our sense of self-worth. Our early environments and connections with our primary caregivers have a big impact on how we view ourselves. Later, it also engages other decision-makers, peers, and other influencers of a similar nature. Our self-esteem is more accurate, the more accurately we see ourselves. When we are young, we begin to internalize how people perceive us, and this becomes our self-perception.

This self-image is severely skewed in many situations and characteristics, which leads to a wide range of behavioral, emotional, and psychological issues. Adults have the freedom to investigate their capacity for self-evaluation and self-perception. Then, we can change the negative and troublesome factors, leading to a rise in self-esteem. Your entire life might be ruined by low self-esteem, and you're unconfident when interacting with people, which make it challenging to build relationships and prosper in social settings. It becomes challenging to maintain a conversation with friends and romantic partners.

Additionally affecting your job and work life is low self-esteem. The fact that you have poor self-esteem even when you are alone is possibly its worst aspect. You doubt your abilities, you negatively judge others and yourself, and you feel insufficient.

Child abuse, physical, verbal, mental, emotional, and sexual, can all contribute to poor self-esteem. The child learns from all of these incidents that their surroundings are not safe. Nothing is reliable. Childhood abuse survivors frequently have to deal with being held accountable for the crimes that were perpetrated against them. True enough, childhood is frequently the foundation of poor self-reasons. You can start to mend the inner small child who needs to regain self-confidence by addressing the deep-rooted traumas to self-image and worldview.

I battled poor self-esteem for years. In other words, I didn't think well of myself. Because I felt unlikable and damaged, I assumed that others did not like me either. I believed I was unlovable and undeserving of love. It was difficult for me to accept compliments. Additionally, my relationships, communication abilities, career prospects, and self- confidence were all impacted by my poor self-esteem. I frequently imagine how different my life might be if I didn't have poor self-esteem.

Due to my poor self-esteem and self-deprecation, I avoided challenges and goal setting and blamed myself for events beyond my control. Without a doubt, I was unable to handle criticism and battled depression for years. Furthermore, when I made a mistake, I became angry. I believed that if someone was upset about something that didn't affect me, I was to blame. I often wished I could just stop everything. I was suffering in silence, appearing to be dead inside but still alive, because of the bad opinion I held of myself. My emotions were wildly shifting. I had to get away from my anxiousness but had no idea how. My poor self-esteem had me on an endless rollercoaster.

But you and I don't have to let having poor self-esteem rule our lives. By reprogramming our cognitive patterns, we can live a successful and content life. As a man thinks, so is he, according to God's word (Proverbs 23;7). In other words, our reality of who we are is shaped by our thoughts and heartfelt tendencies. They influence how we think, which in turn influences how we act. The Bible also says, "The tongue has the power of life and death" (Proverbs 18:21). By the words we speak to ourselves, the tongue can be utilized as a weapon to strengthen, heal, destroy, or harm. By altering our words and thoughts, we can move from hopelessness and gloom to self-love and assurance.

CHAPTER 8

RE DISCOVERING YOURSELF

Strong emotions result from childhood trauma, such as severe neglect or abuse. If you don't deal with those emotions while you're young, they could stick in your head and affect both your conduct and how you feel about yourself. When you process and face the emotions connected to these traumatic memories, you can heal from childhood abuse and learn to love yourself.

It might be challenging to separate as a youngster between your senses of self and how you feel about the trauma you endured. And these emotions grow more difficult to separate when you are allowed to mend on your own. Negative sentiments about yourself, such as guilt, shame, wrath, and fear, can be brought on by childhood trauma and last for a very long time. You are still gifted with time to begin to love yourself. You can learn to love yourself after being abused in childhood, then your confidence will grow.

Recognizing your worth and value is crucial, particularly if you want to have a happy and successful life. You need a lot of self-assurance and a solid feeling of self worth to feel alive. You're more likely to succeed in every area of your life if you continue to believe in yourself. You'll gain confidence in yourself, understand your contribution, take part in more enjoyable activities, and have a clear understanding of your principles.

All of us are capable of gaining self-assurance and having a favorable opinion of ourselves. Everything begins with coming to terms with who you are as a person, embracing and loving yourself, realizing that you don't have to please other people, and accepting complete responsibility. Not only will being confident in yourself enable you to reach your full potential, but it will also significantly improve the quality of your life to help you understand your worth and regain full control over your life. Therefore, the goal is not to find the individual who can solve your problems but to deal with your childhood traumas to discover the real you.

You must first love yourself, exactly as you are, to create a strong, enduring relationship, and you can only achieve this level of self-acceptance by dealing with your past traumas. When we are honest with ourselves, we frequently find that we have gotten into a vicious cycle of believing that the trauma we experienced in the past makes us unfit for a good relationship. This causes us to damage the things we desire by making a self-fulfilling prophecy rooted in our past mistakes, which ruins the relationship we're attempting to establish whether or not it is family, friends, co-workers, or significant others. Accept who you are involved in. Accept your fabulously distinctive qualities, your apparent shortcomings, your abilities, and your boundless potential. Your light is completely distinct from everyone else's and is unlike theirs... as well as characteristics you could consider "flaws" or "hang ups." Instead of viewing past transgressions or tragedies through the prism of self-hatred, think about the lessons you can learn from them and how you can apply them to your life now. "You find peace not by rearranging the circumstances of your life, but by realizing who you are at the deepest level." Eckhart Tolle.

One of the most important steps toward loving yourself is to prioritize your physical and mental well being is committing to practice self care. As a result of feeling inadequate or undeserving of love, many people who experienced abuse as children treat their bodies and brains poorly. Spend time every day concentrating on treating yourself well, regardless of what you think you deserve. Be kind to yourself as you would to a beloved friend. Healthy nutrition, regular exercise, getting adequate sleep, and reducing your stress are all ways to take care of yourself. To see how you are doing, check in with yourself, and then make any necessary improvements. You must first establish your goals for your emotional well being. What causes you to feel angry or hurt? What conditions must be met for you to feel secure? Whatever those things are, you value them because they are important to you. These are what you need. Your requirements should also be respected. It's crucial to communicate your boundaries to others and let them know what you require for them to connect with you. Setting expectations for your interactions with others enables you to build relationships based on trust and ensures that you will be respected.

Make sure others are aware of your boundaries after you have established them for yourself. You can learn to connect with yourself and cherish your interests by engaging in things that make you happy and ignite your passion. When you live a life of constant worry and exhaustion, there is nothing to look forward to. You can feel better about your goals and rediscover your love for yourself by learning to be yourself and accomplish what makes you happy.

Not forgetting the past trauma and abuse you endured to suppress these emotions is not letting go. It is more important to understand that you did not deserve what happened to you, either as a child or as an adult. To start building the life you genuinely want to live; you must learn to let go of the suffering from the past and permit yourself to be free from past wrongs and trauma. The only way you can learn to fully love yourself is to let go and acknowledge that you are prepared to move on.

After experiencing abusive parents as a child, it can take a while to learn to love oneself. Working with a professional counselor or therapist as part of your support system can help you get through your suffering and learn to feel certain and optimistic about the future. "You do not need to travel anywhere. Journey within yourself, enter a mine of rubies, and bathe in the splendor of your light," Rum.

As an adult who experienced abuse as a child, I have viewed myself through damaged lenses and believe that I was unlovable, stupid, and unattractive. Through my eyes, I could see nothing admirable about myself. I had the idea that I needed to be both pretty and smart in order to be liked and accepted. I seemed to be experiencing the same emotions on the inside as I was outside. I walked around dead on the inside and had low self-esteem. I didn't love who I was. How could anyone love me when my mother rejected me as her daughter? I was fighting to survive while in excruciating pain and wandering around dead within. I had been suicidal and miserable for years. I believed I was the worst human being there was. In addition, I permitted others to treat me poorly. I was invisible to everyone, including my family, on a number of occasions, or better yet, for my whole life.

Because I didn't wear name-brand clothing, I would draw strange looks from people. They had no idea that I was in pain and practically dead. Actually, nobody was there to help me. I cried every day, but it didn't stay long since I had to maintain my composure. I was usually solemn and would never smile. I was unsure of how to laugh.

"Change your thoughts and you change your world." Norman Vincent

CHAPTER 9

CHANGING YOUR THOUGHTS

Your life and spirit are permanently changed by traumatic experiences you had as a child. People who experience loss, abuse, or neglect early in life frequently experience severe psychological and emotional illnesses for years and years to come.

This alters who they are and makes it impossible for them to develop loving relationships even long after the painful occurrence. We are held back and have our possibilities blocked in the most unbelievable ways by childhood trauma. It is simpler to build walls when our hearts are wounded during such crucial developmental phases and much more difficult to obtain the healing we seek.

One of the most difficult things we can do is heal the wrongs and hurts from our childhood because doing so is essential if we want to design the life we want. To deal with childhood trauma, you must first understand it. Trauma can trigger painful emotions, and if we do not learn how to manage these emotions, we will continue to repeat the same unhealthy patterns that hold us back and hurt us. The denial of our childhood festers like untreated wounds.

It remains in our bodies as an unconscious energy that destroys everything from our career prospects to romantic relationships. Healing trauma begins with understanding the trauma and the various emotions that accompany it. When you begin to understand your trauma and how it affects you, you can begin to change, but only when you are ready. We continue to be baffled by the human intellect. We know a lot about how it functions, but we still don't fully understand all its annoyances and intricacies. How exactly are we experiencing reality? How is consciousness operative? How are we currently feeling these things in this body? If you pause to consider it for a second, the ideas will intimidate you. We are struggling to comprehend this overwhelming reality because it is so big.

The human brain functions like a pre-programmed computer. In the form of our DNA, it contains some software that is installed at birth, but after that, every new experience is another memory registered, which may produce a range of functions. These activities become habits as we age. However, everything is formed by our thoughts and how we view the world at its most fundamental level. Indeed, every one of us is unique in our own way. Identical twins can develop into radically different individuals as they mature because of the particular manner in which their thoughts develop and affect their lives, this is the case. Human nature and the heavenly chisel are what sculpt us into the people we are. I don't think we will ever fully comprehend it. However, anything is conceivable for those who are able to recognize it and harness their actual power.

You may process anything from 50,000 to as many as 70,000 thoughts in a single day, according to the human mind. Most of such thoughts are undoubtedly unconscious. Not all of those ideas are original, either. Our subconscious minds recycle and repeat a lot of our thoughts. They are a result of our darkest, most primal fears. No matter what we do, we can't seem to escape these 'what-if' scenarios.

One of the most pervasive thoughts in our minds is one based on fear. Thoughts that are grounded in the utmost purity of love, honesty, and forgiveness are on the other extreme of that continuum. Nevertheless, not enough of our ideas are motivated by love. Many of them are founded on fear. Living in a fear-based mindset has the drawback that those fears have a propensity to materialize into reality.

Living in dread puts a strain on your mental, emotional, spiritual, and of course physical health. You waste a lot of mental energy wondering about the worst-case scenarios and focusing on 'what-ifs.' Our thoughts that are motivated by fear frequently concern our finances and relationships, but they can also be about our careers, health, and other aspects of our lives.

Obviously, living in dread for a large portion of the time has a negative impact on your emotional state. Emotions result from thoughts. Any fear-based idea will result in a series of resulting emotions that will provide the groundwork for tension and anxiety. Stress hormones are produced when your emotions are overworked, which not only weighs heavily on your spirit but also severely impacts your body. Your reproductive and digestive systems are suppressed, and your immune system is completely destroyed.

It is very evident how powerful our fear-based thinking is. They may destroy us. They have the power to cause us to race for the ropes and the trenches. Numerous individuals from all over the world are forced to live in a constant state of terror, which is a terrible mental condition to be in. But if you're serious about reaching your objectives or making a significant contribution to the world, you need to free yourself from a fear-based perspective. No matter how challenging it may seem, we must lean toward love. Love is effortless and empowering, whereas fear and hate demand a lot of energy. The sooner you switch from a fear-based to a love-based mindset, the sooner you'll experience the purgative catharsis that comes with unadulterated, unconditional love. Living there will not make you gullible. That's just the natural force of ideas at work all the time in our thoughts. Everybody is a creature of habit. We have strict habits because we've trained ourselves over many years (and even decades) to think, feel, and act in certain ways.

These kinds of ingrained thought patterns can either pave the way for an inspiring and rewarding existence or, over time, contribute to our eventual downfall. Since they serve as the basis for any form of life we may choose to lead, thoughts are actually objects. You must harness the power of your thoughts by changing your way of thinking if you're serious about reaching your objectives and doing anything worthwhile in life. Insanity is defined by Albert Einstein as, "Doing the same thing repeatedly and expecting different results." You can't expect to think, feel, and act one way while getting different outcomes. To achieve significant outcomes, you must take drastic action by sowing the seeds of change.

However, it doesn't happen immediately. There is a path to success for those who are sincere. You can bring your aspirations into reality if you can just change the way you think. How then does this operate? The use of a few fundamental principles to assist you create and attract whatever it is that you desire in your life gave rise to this multi-step procedure. You can do anything as long as you understand the value of concentrated thought and can put these methods into practice.

Your ability to succeed depends on how focused you are. The more you can concentrate your thoughts, the more likely you are to succeed in achieving your goals. You'll struggle to accomplish anything in life if you concentrate on the wrong things. Discover how to focus more intentionally and precisely to lead you in the right route. If you don't, you'll feel more at the mercy of your life's circumstances than in control of them. We may start by altering the way we think. According to the Bible, Philippians 4:8 instruct us to think about things that are genuine, honest, pure, and beautiful things that are of good report. I still struggle to restrain my thoughts.

Though it is a daily battle, I am improving at thinking positively. In order to stop thinking negatively about my mistreatment and abuse, I've been working with my inner child. I try very hard not to think negatively, even when things happen to me at work. I occasionally fail because I let some thoughts control me, especially when I'm not chosen for anything. I try to justify my rejection to myself, but that doesn't work for me being the type I am, I consider the whole circumstance. But as it turns out, it causes more harm than benefit. I must let it go. Remember, healing is processes so don’t be hard on yourself.

THE END....

Made in the USA
Middletown, DE
21 October 2024

62574510R00044